Usborne Better English

Grammar &
Punctuation

Written by
Sam Taplin

Designed by
Pete Taylor

Cover illustration by
Alex Latimer

Contents

About this book

Grammar and **punctuation** sometimes seem like confusing things designed to make English difficult. In fact, they're the opposite: they are vital tools that can help you. If you learn a few **simple rules**, you'll be able to **read** and **write** more confidently.

In this book you'll find **50 exercises** to help you learn. There are **explanations** of tricky grammar points, **guides** on how to use different punctuation marks, and examples of some **common mistakes** to avoid.

What is grammar?

Grammar is simply the way you use **words** to build **sentences** that everyone can **understand**. You use grammar every time you say anything – so you already know quite a lot about it, even if you don't think you do. For example, if you read this...

The gorilla big very was.

...then you probably know that the words ought to be in this order:

The gorilla was very big.

Learning the rules of grammar will help to stop your writing from being confusing or difficult to follow. In this book you'll **learn how to use words correctly** and put them together so that your **meaning is clear**.

What is punctuation?

Punctuation is the set of little **symbols**, such as commas, question marks and full stops, that you use to **break up writing and make it easier to read**. Look how difficult it is to read this, with no punctuation at all:

> *Ill ask Merlin a very powerful wizard to make the monster disappear she said.*

You can probably work out what it means after a while, but look how much easier it is with punctuation added:

> *"I'll ask Merlin, a very powerful wizard, to make the monster disappear," she said.*

Punctuation shows where sentences begin, pause, and end, and it shows when someone's talking. Knowing how to use it will **make your writing much clearer**.

How to use this book

In each two-page section of this book you'll learn about **one new subject** and then get the chance to **test yourself** with an exercise. Then you can **check your answers** and read more about that topic.

It's a good idea to **go through the exercises in order**, because you'll gradually learn more and build up to the slightly tougher tasks later in the book. If you like, you can **write your answers in pencil** so you can rub them out and try again if you go wrong.

If you want to go straight to a particular topic, you'll find an **index of grammar and punctuation words** at the back, as well as a summary of the main topics.

To test your knowledge with lots of puzzles, activities and games, go to:

www.usborne.com/quicklinks

and type the keywords "English grammar".

Spot the verbs

A verb is a word, such as "dance", "shine", "think" or "promise", that tells you what someone or something is doing. Every sentence has to have a verb in it.

Which of these are verbs? Circle each one, then turn the page to check.

orange   queen

(juggle)   (sing)

peculiar   (follow)

brilliant   (crazy)

(eat)   (enjoy) (be)

(disappear) kangaroo

Spot the verbs

If you're wondering if a word is a verb, see if you can put "I" or "to" in front of it: you can say "I enjoy" or "to juggle" so you know "enjoy" and "juggle" are verbs, but you can't say "I kangaroo" or "to crazy", so those aren't verbs. Some verbs (called "irregular verbs") don't follow the rules: you can't say "I be" but "be" is still a verb.

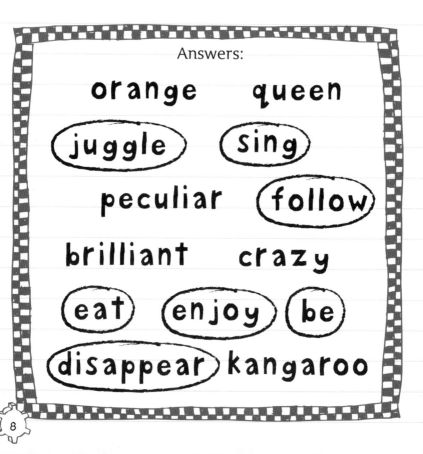

Answers:

orange   queen

(juggle)   (sing)

peculiar   (follow)

brilliant   crazy

(eat) (enjoy) (be)

(disappear) kangaroo

Find the subjects

The subject is whoever or whatever
is doing the action in a sentence.

The weasel nibbled my toes.

Here, the weasel is the subject because it's
doing the action – nibbling. (The person or
thing the action is happening to is called
the object – see page 11.)

Circle the subject of each sentence.

(I) like marzipan.

(Gulwant) flies planes.

(The chair) fell to pieces.

(Jack) paints pictures.

(My) dad baked a cake.

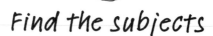

Find the subjects

The subject of a sentence usually comes near the start, followed by the verb and then the object:

Sarah painted the picture.

In this sentence, the subject (Sarah) is at the beginning, the verb (painted) comes next, and the object (the picture) comes at the end.

Answers:

(I) like marzipan.

(Gulwant) flies planes.

(The chair) fell to pieces.

(Jack) paints pictures.

(My dad) baked a cake.

Spot the objects

The object is the person or thing that the verb of a sentence is happening to.

Jessica climbed the ladder.

The ladder is the object because the verb ("climb") is happening to the ladder. (The person or thing doing the action is the subject – see page 9.)

Circle the object of these sentences.

Peter has two cats.

All of a sudden, he heard a piercing scream.

The gorilla frightened Mrs Wiggins.

He cleaned the boots.

11

Spot the objects

The object of a sentence usually comes near the end. The subject usually comes first, then the verb, then the object:

The monkey ate the cake.

In this sentence, the subject (the monkey) comes right at the start, then the verb (ate) and then finally the object (the cake).

Answers:

Peter has (two cats.)

All of a sudden, he heard (a piercing scream.)

The gorilla frightened (Mrs Wiggins.)

He cleaned (the boots.)

Spot the nouns

A noun is a word that tells you the name of something: "boat", "Paris", "zebra" and "Mrs Baggio" are all nouns. A noun can be a person, an animal, a thing or a place.

Circle all the nouns in these sentences. There's more than one noun in each one. Turn over to check your answers.

A giraffe wearing skates went whizzing past our school.

At the top of the mountain, Sir Harry met a huge dragon and a beautiful princess.

A purple alien sat in his rocket, singing a happy song.

13

Spot the nouns

If you can put "a", "an" or "the" in front of a word, the word is a noun. For example, you can say "an alien", "the giraffe" or "the skates", so "alien", "giraffe" and "skates" are nouns. But you can't say "a whizzing", "the went" or "an our", so you know that "whizzing", "went" and "our" are not nouns.

Answers:

A giraffe wearing skates went whizzing past our school.

At the top of the mountain, Sir Harry met a huge dragon and a beautiful princess.

A purple alien sat in his rocket, singing a happy song.

Proper nouns

A proper noun is the name of one particular person or thing. The names of people and places (such as "Roberta" or "New York") are proper nouns and so are the names of months and days.

Which of these nouns are proper nouns? Circle each one.

birthday

Stephanie

monkey

envelope

December

magician

Tuesday

computer

Elvis Presley

Paris

America

cheesecake

Sherlock Holmes

Proper nouns

Proper nouns start with a capital letter:

Yesterday I met the secret agent in Odesa. Her name is Christine Diamond.

"Odesa" starts with a capital letter because it's the name of a place. "Christine Diamond" also has capital letters because it's someone's name.

Answers:

birthday **(Stephanie)**

monkey envelope

(December) magician

(Tuesday) computer

(Elvis Presley) **(Paris)**

(America) cheesecake

(Sherlock Holmes)

Spot the pronouns

A pronoun is any word that replaces a noun in a sentence. For example, you can say "she" instead of "Miss Singh". "She" is replacing a proper noun (Miss Singh), so it's a pronoun.

Which of these words are pronouns? Draw a circle around each one.

(he)   beach   (we)

playing   when

spaghetti   (him)

(them)   goldfish

(it's)   circus   (they)

knife   finished   (it)

Spot the pronouns

To decide if a word is a pronoun, ask yourself, "Does it stand for a noun?"

Jon knew that Kate would be surprised when she saw the flowers.

Here "she" is a pronoun, because it stands for "Kate".

Answers:

(he)   beach   (we)

playing   when

spaghetti   (him)

(them)   goldfish

it's   circus   (they)

knife   finished   (it)

Using pronouns

Repeating the same noun in a sentence often sounds awkward. You can use pronouns to avoid repeating yourself and make the sentence flow better.

Make these sentences sound better by changing nouns into pronouns.

My sister loves ice cream.
~~My sister~~ _She_ says
~~ice cream~~ _it_ is the most
delicious food ~~my sister~~ _She_
has ever tasted.

Mr Brown stared at the lion
as ~~the lion~~ _it_ padded
towards ~~Mr Brown~~ _him_.

Using pronouns

When it's clear which noun you're referring to, a pronoun is usually best:

My teacher is clever – she knows everything!

This sounds odd without the pronoun:

My teacher is clever – my teacher knows everything!

Answers:

My sister loves ice cream. ~~My sister~~ _She_ says ~~ice cream~~ _it_ is the most delicious food ~~my sister~~ _she_ has ever tasted.

Mr Brown stared at the lion as ~~the lion~~ _it_ padded towards ~~Mr Brown~~ _him_.

"I" or "me"?

In some sentences it's difficult to choose between the pronouns "I" and "me". People often use the wrong one.

Complete these sentences by adding either "I" or "me".

Matt is good friends with Jo and _Me_ .

My dog and _Me_ were running through the park.

Dad built a tree house for my sister and _Me_ .

Ella and _I_ are friends.

"I" or "me"?

Always use "I" when it's the subject of the sentence (see page 9).

I like cheese. (NOT "Me like cheese.")

Always use "me" when it's the object (page 11) or after a preposition (page 55).

Matt is good friends with Jo and ___me___.

My dog and ___I___ were running through the park.

Dad built a tree house for my sister and ___me___.

Ella and ___I___ are friends.

Spot the adjectives

An adjective is a word such as "tall", "red", "angry", "brave" or "shiny" which describes a noun. It answers the question, "What is it like?"

Which of these words are adjectives? Circle each one.

(beautiful)   dinosaur

(green)   parachute

slightly   (delicious)

persuade   soup

guitar   flowers

(hungry)   (brilliant)

Spot the adjectives

Adjectives usually go before a noun:

a happy smile

a giant hamster

But sometimes they don't:

My new kite is big and red.

Answers:

(beautiful) dinosaur

(green) parachute

slightly (delicious)

persuade soup

guitar flowers

(hungry) (brilliant)

Adding adjectives

Adjectives are describing words.
(See page 23 for more about them.)

Complete these phrases by choosing
the most suitable adjective from the list.
Circle the four words in the list that are
not adjectives.

(smell)   funny   sharp   (giggled)

(recipe)   (quickly)   speedy   smelly

When I chop carrots I always

use a ___Sharp___ **knife.**

The monster had extremely

___Smelly___ **breath.**

We all laughed when we heard

the ___funny___ **story.**

Adding adjectives

It's easy to get mixed up between adjectives and adverbs, especially with adjectives such as "friendly" and "prickly" that seem like adverbs because they end in "-ly". See page 29 for more on adverbs.

Answers:

~~smell~~	funny	sharp	~~giggled~~
~~recipe~~	~~quickly~~	speedy	smelly

When I chop carrots I always use a _sharp_ knife.

The monster had extremely _smelly_ breath.

We all laughed when we heard the _funny_ story.

Possessive adjectives

Possessive adjectives are words such as "my" and "your" which show who something belongs to. For example:

This is my house.

Here, "my" is a possessive adjective which tells you more about the house: who it belongs to.

Circle the possessive adjectives.

our   he   its

his   they

them   her

your

him   their

Possessive adjectives

"Its" is a possessive adjective meaning "belonging to it":

The snail peeped out of its shell.

Here the word "its" is an adjective telling you more about the shell – that it belongs to the snail.

It's very easy to get "its" mixed up with the contraction "it's", which is short for "it is" – see page 99.

Circle the possessive adjectives.

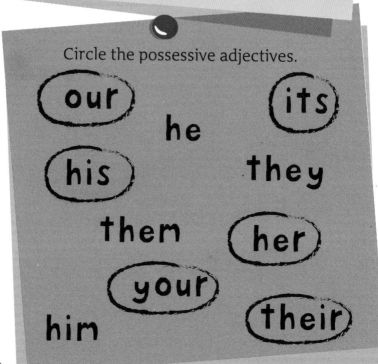

(our)   he   (its)

(his)   they

them   (her)

(your)

him   (their)

Spot the adverbs

An adverb is a word such as "busily" or "quickly" that tells you more about another word in a sentence. Most adverbs tell you how a verb is done. So, in the phrase ...

The bird flew swiftly through the air.

... the adverb is "swiftly" because it describes how the bird flew.

Which of these words are adverbs? Circle each one.

until   enormous

(slowly)   important

hopping   (quietly)

(sleepily)   lucky

(angrily)   whistled

Spot the adverbs

Adverbs can tell you about other words as well as verbs. For example:

You look very different with that hairstyle.

Here, "very" is an adverb that tells you about an adjective – "different". Adverbs can modify any word except a noun. Most adverbs in English end in "-ly". But don't confuse adverbs with adjectives (such as "friendly") that also end in "-ly".

Answers:

until   enormous

slowly   important

hopping   **quietly**

sleepily   lucky

angrily   whistled

Adding adverbs

You can test yourself on adverbs below.
(See page 29 for adverbs.)

Choose the most suitable adverb from the
list to complete each sentence. Circle the
words that are not adverbs.

(tight)   happily   (mysterious)   eerily

(sensational)   (quiet)   angrily   (glad)

The wind whistled ___eerily___

and the door creaked open.

The old man bellowed

___angrily___ at the naughty dog.

She giggled ___happily___ when

she heard the good news.

Adding adverbs

Some words can be either adjectives or adverbs, depending on how they're used:

She tried hard. Here "hard" is an adverb.

The exam was hard. Here it's an adjective.

Answers:

~~tight~~   happily   ~~mysterious~~   eerily
~~sensational~~   ~~quiet~~   angrily   ~~glad~~

The wind whistled ___eerily___ and the door creaked open.

The old man bellowed ___angrily___ at the naughty dog.

She giggled ___happily___ when she heard the good news.

Comparatives and superlatives

Comparatives are adjectives you use when you want to compare two people or things. You usually make an adjective into a comparative adjective by adding "er" to the end: "faster", "lower", "smarter", for example.

Superlatives are adjectives for when you want to compare three or more people or things. You usually make an adjective into a superlative adjective by adding "est" to the end and putting "the" in front of it: "the fastest", "the lowest", "the smartest", for example.

Complete this sentence by adding a comparative and a superlative.

The monkey is loud and the gorilla is even _louder_, but the lion is _the loudest_.

ANSWERS

Comparatives and superlatives

If an adjective ends in "e", just add "r" for the comparative and "st" for the superlative:

large larger largest

If an adjective ends in "y", you change the "y" into an "i" before adding "er" and "est":

happy happier happiest

Some adjectives double their final letter before you add "er" and "est":

thin thinner thinnest

See page 35 for more about comparatives and superlatives.

Answers:

The monkey is loud and the gorilla is even _____louder_____, but the lion is _the loudest_.

Irregular comparatives and superlatives

Some of the most common adjectives, such as "good" and "bad", are irregular and don't follow the normal rules when you make them into comparatives and superlatives. (See page 33 for the normal rules.)

Complete these sentences.

The first book was good and the second one was even _betler_, but the third one was _the best_.

Josh has little money and Millie has even _more_, but Ben has _the most_.

Irregular comparatives and superlatives

Adjectives longer than two syllables don't follow the normal rules either. It sounds odd to say "even amazinger" or "the amazingest" so you say "more amazing" and "the most amazing" instead.

Pippa is a beautiful dog, and Roxy is even more beautiful, but Bella is the most beautiful dog of all.

Answers:

The first book was good and the second one was even ___better___, but the third one was ___the best___.

Josh has little money and Millie has even ___less___, but Ben has ___the least___.

Verbs: infinitives

The name of a verb is called the infinitive. "Chase", "eat" and "climb" are infinitives. When they're used in a sentence, infinitives usually have "to" in front of them, but not always.

Complete these sentences using the infinitives below. Some of them need "to" and some don't.

to do	to read	to wear

Deepak loves *to read* adventure stories.

Claire wasn't sure which dress *to wear.*

My dad said I should *do* my homework.

Verbs: infinitives

If you're not sure whether to include "to" with an infinitive, just say the sentence to yourself – it's usually quite obvious. For example, see how wrong this sentence sounds:

Jess said she might to arrive at the party a little late.

Answers:

Deepak loves *to read* adventure stories.

Claire wasn't sure which dress *to wear* .

My dad said I should *do* my homework.

Verbs: present simple tense

You use verbs in the present simple tense to talk about something that often happens or usually happens. For example:

Lara plays netball every Saturday.

Use the verbs below to complete these sentences with the present simple tense.

> to cast   to fly   to travel

**When I go to Scotland, I always
_____travel_____ by train.**

**Every morning, Wes the Wizard
_____casts_____ a different spell.**

**The eagles _____fly_____ across
the mountains every night.**

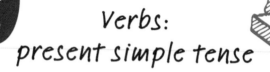

Verbs:
present simple tense

You can also use the present simple tense to talk about things that are going to happen in the future. For example:

We arrive at six.

This could mean, "We will arrive at six." There's more than one form of the present tense. See page 41 to find out about the present continuous tense.

▭ ▭ ▭ ▭ ▭ ▭ ▭ ▭ ▭ ▭ ▭ ▭ ▭

Answers:

When I go to Scotland, I always __travel__ by train.

Every morning, Wes the Wizard __casts__ a different spell.

The eagles __fly__ across the mountains every night.

▭ ▭ ▭ ▭ ▭ ▭ ▭ ▭ ▭ ▭ ▭ ▭ ▭

40

Verbs:
present continuous tense

You use verbs in the present continuous tense when you want to talk about something that's happening right now. For example:

The yeti is eating my shoes.

Complete the sentences using the verbs below in the present continuous tense.

to wear	to do	to play

Emma and Hannah _are_
Playing **chess.**

Anna _is wearing_ **her new gloves.**

You _did_ **well.**

Verbs:
present continuous tense

You can also use the present continuous tense to talk about something that's definitely going to happen soon:

I am flying to Brazil tomorrow morning.

We are leaving at six o'clock.

There's more than one form of the present tense. See page 39 to find out about the present simple tense.

Answers:

Emma and Hannah <u>*are*</u> <u>*playing*</u> chess.

Anna <u>*is wearing*</u> her new gloves.

You <u>*are doing*</u> well.

Verbs:
past simple tense

You use the past simple tense to talk about things that have happened. For most verbs, you make this tense by adding "ed" or "d", so for "play" it's "played" and for "recite" it's "recited".

Complete the sentences using the verbs below in the past simple tense.

to climb   to wish   to finish

Ashwin and Louise
climbed the mountain.

Max was exhausted when he
finished the race.

They _wished_ it could
go on forever.

Verbs:
past simple tense

Some very common verbs don't follow the normal rules when you make the past tense. For example, you don't say:

She buyed the car.

You have to learn what the correct past tense of each of these verbs is. They are called "irregular" verbs and you can find out more about them on the opposite page.

Answers:

Ashwin and Louise _climbed_ the mountain.

Max was exhausted when he _finished_ the race.

They _wished_ it could go on forever.

Verbs: past simple tense of irregular verbs

Many of the most common verbs are "irregular" in the past tense – this means you have to learn their past tense instead of following the normal rules.

Can you think of the past tense of the irregular verbs below? Use the verbs to complete these sentences.

| to fall | to buy | to break | to fight |

I drew my sword and _____ the pirate captain.

Rocco _bought_ bread and fish at the supermarket.

I _broke_ my phone when I _fell_ off the sofa.

Verbs: past simple tense of irregular verbs

Some irregular past tenses follow the same pattern:

throw	threw
grow	grew
Know	Knew

This makes them easier to remember, but lots of verbs that sound similar ("show", "glow", "flow") are actually regular, so you have to learn which are the irregular ones.

Answers:

I drew my sword and **fought** the pirate captain.

Rocco **bought** bread and fish at the supermarket.

I **broke** my phone when I **fell** off the sofa.

Verbs:
past continuous tense

You use the past continuous tense to talk about something that was happening and hadn't finished yet, rather than something that happened. For example:

I was cleaning the window.

Complete the sentences using the verbs below in the past continuous tense.

> to think   to look

He sneaked off while they _were looking_ **the other way.**

You didn't hear what I said because you _were thinking_ **about something else.**

Verbs: past continuous tense

The past continuous tense is often used to describe something that was happening when something else happened:

While I was washing my car, a spaceship landed in my garden.

When they were walking to the station, it started to rain.

Here, "was washing" and "were walking" show that these things were still happening at the moment when the second thing took place.

Answers:

He sneaked off while they **were looking** the other way.

You didn't hear what I said because you **were thinking** about something else.

Verbs: past tense

On this page you'll need to use a mixture
of different past tenses (pages 43-48).

Change all the verbs in this paragraph
so that it's written in the past tense.

Jenny _____woke_____ up,
    (wakes)

_____streched_____ and _____yawned_____,
    (stretches)   (yawns)

then _____sprouted_____ out of bed.
        (springs)

While she _____was brushing_____
                    (is brushing)

her teeth she _____began_____
                    (begins)

to think about the busy day

ahead. Then she _____walked_____
                        (walks)

into the kitchen where

she _____found_____ an alligator
        (finds)

on the table.

Verbs: past tense

Use the past simple tense (page 43) to talk about something that happened at a particular time. Use the past continuous (page 47) to talk about what was happening when something else happened.

Answers:

Jenny **woke** up,
(wakes)
stretched and **yawned**,
(stretches)   (yawns)
then **sprang** out of bed.
(springs)
While she **was brushing**
(is brushing)
her teeth she **began**
(begins)
to think about the busy day
ahead. Then she **walked**
(walks)
into the kitchen where
she **found** an alligator
(finds)
on the table.

Transitive and intransitive verbs

Verbs are used either transitively or intransitively. When you use a verb transitively it only makes sense if it has an object – if the verb is being done to something or someone. "Blame" is a transitive verb because you can't just say, "I blame". It needs an object:

I blame the government.

"Rise" is an intransitive verb because it never has an object. You can't "rise" someone or something and you always use the verb on its own.

Can you circle the transitive verbs?

die   glow   (destroy)

thank   (enjoy)   (wear)

flow   (prefer) hover

Transitive and intransitive verbs

Lots of verbs can be either transitive or intransitive, depending on how they're used. For example:

The plane flew very fast.

Here the verb "fly" is being used intransitively because it doesn't have an object: the plane isn't "flying" something or someone, it's just flying.

The pilot flew the plane very fast.

Here "fly" is transitive because it has an object: the pilot is flying the plane.

Answers:

die   **glow**   **destroy**

thank   **enjoy**   **wear**

flow   **prefer**   **hover**

Verbs: list of tenses

Verbs can be used in lots of different tenses. Pages 39-49 describe some of the most useful ones in detail.

Here's a list of all the tenses:

Present simple .... *I dance.*
Present continuous .. *I am dancing.*
Present perfect .... *I have danced.*
Present perfect
continuous .... *I have been dancing.*

Past simple .... *I danced.*
Past continuous .... *I was dancing.*
Past perfect .... *I had danced.*
Past perfect
continuous .... *I had been dancing.*

Future simple .... *I will dance.*
Future continuous ... *I will be dancing.*
Future perfect .... *I will have danced.*
Future perfect
continuous .... *I will have been dancing.*

Verbs: list of tenses

Draw a line from each verb tense to the correct sentence. Check the previous page to see if you've got them right.

Present simple   *I had been dancing.*

Present continuous   *I will be dancing.*

Present perfect   *I will have danced.*

Present perfect
continuous   *I had danced.*

Past simple   *I dance.*

Past continuous   *I danced.*

Past perfect   *I have been dancing.*

Past perfect
continuous

Future simple   *I will dance.*

Future continuous   *I have danced.*

Future perfect   *I will have been dancing.*

Future perfect
continuous   *I am dancing.*

                           I was dancing.

Spot the prepositions

Prepositions are words such as "in" and "on" that show you the relationship between two things. They often tell you where one thing is in relation to another.

There are nine prepositions in the following paragraph. Circle them all.

John crawled under the gate and into the overgrown park. He spotted a fox hiding among the bushes, a rabbit near the bench and a deer behind a tree. He climbed up the stone steps, tiptoed past the statue, and sneaked across the grass. Then he hid inside the shed.

Spot the prepositions

A preposition always comes before a noun.

The monkey climbed up the tree.

Here "up" is the preposition because it tells you about the relationship between the monkey and tree.

Answers:

John crawled under the gate and into the overgrown park. He spotted a fox hiding among the bushes, a rabbit near the bench and a deer behind a tree. He climbed up the stone steps, tiptoed past the statue, and sneaked across the grass. Then he hid inside the shed.

The passive voice

The window was smashed by the ball.

The sentence above is written in the "passive voice". This means that the subject of the sentence (the window) is having the action done to it. We usually use the active voice, which would be:

The ball smashed the window.

Rewrite these sentences in the passive voice.

Sophie played the guitar.

The guitar was played by Sophie.

The mouse ate the cheese.

The cheese was eaten by the mouse.

The passive voice

Because the passive voice is less direct than the active voice, it's often used to make sentences sound less aggressive:

Smoking is not permitted.

This sounds less abrupt than:

Do not smoke.

It's also useful when you're not sure who did something:

The diamonds have been stolen!

Answers:

Sophie played the guitar.

The guitar was played by Sophie.

The mouse ate the cheese.

The cheese was eaten by the mouse.

Sentences

A sentence is a group of words that makes sense on its own.

I like swimming.

This is a sentence because you don't need any other words to make sense of it.

When I go swimming

This is not a sentence, because it doesn't make sense on its own.

Which of these are sentences? Add full stops to the sentences and circle the ones that aren't sentences.

He strode across the room.

The robot beeped when it

I haven't seen her for years.

I like apples, pears

Sentences

A sentence usually has a subject (page 9), a verb (page 7) and an object (page 11).

Daisy rides horses.

"Daisy" is the subject, "rides" is the verb and "horses" is the object. Some sentences don't seem to follow this rule:

Does Daisy ride horses? Yes.

"Yes" is a sentence here, but only because the other sentence explains it. It means:

Yes, Daisy rides horses.

Answers:

He strode across the room.

The robot beeped when it

I haven't seen her for years.

I like apples, pears

Full stops

A full stop is the dot at the end of a sentence. It marks a break between two sentences: if you're reading out loud, you should leave a definite pause when you get to a full stop. After a full stop, the next sentence starts with a capital letter.

Rewrite each line of words as sentences, adding full stops and capital letters.

i have a pet dragon it lives in the shed

I have a pet dragon.

It lives in the shed.

my sister loves football she plays it every day

My sister loves frootball.

She plays it every day.

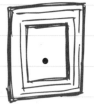

Full stops

Remember – you only use a full stop after a sentence. So if a sign says ...

NO ENTRY

... there's no full stop because it's not a sentence.

Full stops are used for abbreviations (short forms of words). For example, you can use "m.p.h." instead of "miles per hour".

Answers:

i have a pet dragon it lives in the shed

I have a pet dragon.
It lives in the shed.

my sister loves football she plays it every day

My sister loves football.
She plays it every day.

Commas

A comma stands for a short pause that separates a word or a group of words from the rest of a sentence. Commas are often essential to make the meaning of a sentence clear. Look at this sentence:

We ate chocolate ice cream and trifle.

And now see how the meaning changes if you add a comma:

We ate chocolate, ice cream and trifle.

Add one comma to each of these sentences to change the meaning.

In the chest she found gold, necklaces and jewels.

I like drawing, cars and trains.

Cyclists, don't use this lane.

Commas

Notice how you can completely change the meaning of a word by adding or removing a comma. In this sentence ...

Would you like coffee, cake or apple crumble?

... the word "coffee" is a noun, and you're being given three choices. But if you remove the comma, "coffee" becomes an adjective describing the cake, and you're only being offered two different things.

See pages 65-74 for more about commas.

Answers:

In the chest she found gold, necklaces and jewels.

I like drawing, cars and trains.

Cyclists, don't use this lane.

Commas in lists

When a sentence has a list, each item is separated from the next by a comma:

I've been to Sweden, Italy, France and Germany.

As you can see above, the last word in the list is usually joined to the list by "and" instead of a comma.

Add commas to these lists so that they make sense:

The room was big, dark, cold and empty.

He put nuts, sugar, flour, eggs and butter into the mixture.

She hopped, skipped, jumped and clapped her hands.

Commas in lists

There are some lists where you need to put a comma before the "and":

My dogs are called Banjo, Billie, Jack, Thunder, and Lightning.

This sentence describes five dogs. But without the last comma you might think there were only four dogs, the fourth one being called "Thunder and Lightning".

Answers:

The room was big, dark, cold and empty.

He put nuts, sugar, flour, eggs and butter into the mixture.

She hopped, skipped, jumped and clapped her hands.

Commas before conjunctions

Long sentences usually need a comma to make them clearer. The comma often comes before a conjunction, or joining word, such as "but", "until" or "although":

She waited outside the cinema for half an hour, but her friend was stuck in traffic and didn't turn up.

Make these sentences clearer by adding one comma to each.

The bull snorted and began to charge, so they ran through the gate and out of the field.

She's the best dancer I've ever seen, but yesterday she fell over in the middle of a spin.

Commas before conjunctions

Some of the most common words that are used as conjunctions are:

after, before, until, while, since, if, unless, though, as, for, but, although, and, until, so

Whenever you use one of these words in the middle of a sentence, think about whether you need a comma to separate one part of the sentence from the other.

Answers:

The bull snorted and began to charge, so they ran through the gate and out. of the field.

She's the best dancer I've ever seen, but yesterday she fell over in the middle of a spin.

Clauses

A sentence is sometimes made up of one main part (a main clause) and other, less important parts (subordinate clauses). A main clause could work as a sentence on its own, but a subordinate clause needs a main clause in order to make sense:

She showed me her new painting, which was beautiful.

"She showed me her new painting" could be a sentence on its own, so it's the main clause. But "which was beautiful" couldn't be a sentence on its own, so it's a subordinate clause.

Circle the main clause of this sentence.

She raised her eyebrows when the tiger jumped through the window.

Clauses

A main clause can sometimes be a lot shorter than the subordinate clause:

When she saw the man running down the street shouting, "There's a rhinoceros in my garden!" and waving his arms in the air, Laura frowned.

In the above sentence, "Laura frowned" is actually the main clause, even though it's much shorter than the long subordinate clause at the start. Although it's very long, the first part of the sentence couldn't be a sentence on its own – but this could:

Laura frowned.

Answers:

She raised her eyebrows when the tiger jumped through the window.

Commas with clauses

A subordinate clause (see page 69) is often separated from the main clause of a sentence by a comma. The comma helps to make the sentence clearer and simpler. Notice how this sentence ...

Crocodiles have sharp teeth,which makes them dangerous.

... is easier to read with a comma separating the clauses:

Crocodiles have sharp teeth, which makes them dangerous.

Add a comma between the clauses of each sentence to make it easier to read.

I ate fifteen cakes, which made me feel peculiar.

She loved ice-skating, though she wasn't very good at it.

Commas with clauses

Remember that subordinate clauses can come anywhere in a sentence, not just at the end. If you're not sure which is the main clause, just ask yourself which part of the sentence could work as a sentence on its own:

She loved ice-skating

... could be a sentence. So it's the main clause.

though she wasn't very good at it

... couldn't, so it's a subordinate clause.

Answers:

I ate fifteen cakes, which made me feel peculiar.

She loved ice-skating, though she wasn't very good at it.

Commas and meaning

The meaning of a sentence can be changed completely if you add or remove commas.

The soldiers, who had fought all day, went home.

This means all the soldiers fought all day.

The soldiers who had fought all day went home.

Now it means that only some of the soldiers had fought all day, and they were the ones who went home.

Add two commas to each sentence to change its meaning.

The boat, which was leaking, began to sink.

The desserts, which had apples in them, were delicious.

Commas and meaning

Taking one comma out of a sentence, rather than a pair of commas, can still change the meaning totally. (See page 63 for more about this.) For example:

He threw away the eggs, which were broken.

He threw away the eggs which were broken.

She loved the kittens, which were black and white.

She loved the kittens which were black and white.

Answers:

The boat, which was leaking, began to sink.

The desserts, which had apples in them, were delicious.

Question marks

A question mark is used at the end of a sentence which asks a question. Question sentences often begin with question words: "Why", "When", "Where", "Who", "Which" or "How".

Add question marks after the questions and full stops after the other sentences.

When did you find out that your dad was a superhero?

When we come home from school, we have a snack.

Where is the science museum?

Where I live, there's a big field with horses in it.

Question marks

Notice that some sentences starting with "When," "Where" and so on are not questions. Also remember that questions can be tagged onto the end of a sentence:

I think we can get there tonight, can't we?

Answers:

When did you find out that your dad was a superhero?

When we come home from school, we have a snack.

Where is the science museum?

Where I live, there's a big field with horses in it.

Exclamation marks

You can use an exclamation mark at the end of a sentence to show that the sentence expresses a strong feeling, such as anger, joy, surprise or fear. It makes it sound more emphatic:

The gun was pointing straight at me!

But it's never essential to use an exclamation mark – you could always use a full stop instead. Using too many will make your writing less effective.

Only one of these exclamation marks is really appropriate. Circle the others.

I had a very peaceful day!

I've never been so happy!

It was quite boring at the zoo!

She went into the shop!

Exclamation marks

You never need to use more than one exclamation mark at once. In this sentence ...

It was really amazing!!!

... a single exclamation mark would get the point across just as well.

It can also spoil your writing if you keep using them. This story would be more effective with fewer exclamation marks:

I saw the monster! It was huge! It was coming towards me! I couldn't escape!

Answers:

I had a very peaceful day!

I've never been so happy!

It was quite boring at the zoo!

She went into the shop!

Apostrophes to show possession

An apostrophe can be used to show who or what something belongs to:

Imran's shoes
The ladies' hats
The men's coats

As you can see above, if the owner is singular (like Imran), you put an apostrophe at the end, then add "s". If the owners are plural and end in "s" (like ladies), you just add an apostrophe after the "s". If the owners are plural but don't end in "s" (like men), you add an apostrophe followed by an "s".

Add an apostrophe in the correct position in these phrases, and an "s" if needed.

The book's pages

The children's books

The girls' jackets

Apostrophes to show possession

If you're not sure whether a noun with an "s" needs an apostrophe, try using "of". For example, instead of this ...

Rachel's scarf

... you can say this:

The scarf of Rachel

This means it's possessive, so it needs 's.

If the owner is singular but the name ends in "s" (like Seamus), you can use an apostrophe and "s" as usual, or you can just use the apostrophe:

Seamus's bicycle OR Seamus' bicycle

Answers:

The book's pages

The children's books

The girls' jackets

Apostrophes for contractions

Apostrophes can be used to fill in for missing letters in a word (contractions):

she has = she's
you are = you're
I am = I'm

The apostrophe goes wherever the letter or letters have been removed.

Write these sentences with apostrophes.

Im good at climbing, but youre even better.

I'm good at climbing, but you're even better

Hes not here, so weve phoned him.

He's not here, so we've phoned him.

Apostrophes for contractions

Here are a few tricky contractions:

shall not = shan't
I would = I'd
I had = I'd
will not = won't
of the clock = o'clock

Notice how "shan't" and "won't" are more complicated – letters have been removed, but not only where the apostrophe is.

Answers:

Im good at climbing, but youre even better.

I'm good at climbing, but you're even better.

Hes not here, so weve phoned him.

He's not here, so we've phoned him.

Colons

A colon is used to introduce something that follows. It can be a list, like this:

You will need: vinegar, olive oil and salt.

Or it can be when the second half of a sentence explains or expands on the first half of the sentence:

Finally he told us the secret: he had stolen the painting and hidden it.

Add a colon in the correct place in each sentence.

Please bring the following: a warm coat, walking boots, a packed lunch and a compass.

Then, at last, I discovered the truth: my friend was a spy!

Colons

Here are some phrases which are quite often followed by a colon. Whenever you use one of these phrases in your writing, think about whether you might need to put a colon afterwards.

for example
in other words
the following
as follows
namely

Answers:

Please bring the following: a warm coat, walking boots, a packed lunch and a compass.

Then, at last, I discovered the truth: my friend was a spy!

Semi-colons

A semi-colon marks a fairly long pause; it's longer than a comma but shorter than a full stop. It's used to link two sentences which are connected in meaning and equally important. The semi-colon helps to show that the two points are linked:

My mum loves playing tennis; my dad prefers badminton.

He peered inside the house; the stranger was inside.

Add one semi-colon to each sentence so that it makes sense.

We arrived late at the party even so, we had a great time.

He opened the box the gleam of gold was visible inside.

Semi-colons

Semi-colons are sometimes useful for dividing up the entries in long lists, especially when the items in the lists are long and complicated:

To make your kite you will need: one metre of thick, strong string; two long, wooden poles; one large sheet of sturdy paper; and finally, markers, paint or crayons to decorate it.

All the semi-colons above could be commas, but it would be harder to read.

Remember that you don't put a capital letter after a semi-colon.

Answers:

We arrived late at the party; even so, we had a great time.

He opened the box; the gleam of gold was visible inside.

Brackets

Brackets are used around a group of words to keep them separate from the rest of the sentence:

I spoke to my friend Jasmine (who's a doctor) about my sore foot.

The information in brackets adds something to the sentence, but the sentence should still make sense if you remove the bracketed section:

I spoke to my friend Jasmine about my sore foot.

Complete these sentences by adding brackets:

Her brother who arrived today is coming tonight .

I like rock music especially The Flying Saucers .

Brackets

If the words between brackets aren't a complete sentence, punctuation marks go outside the brackets:

I'll come to see you tomorrow (in the afternoon), because I'm busy today (with work).

If the words inside the brackets are a complete sentence, the punctuation mark goes inside the brackets:

I'm getting up at five o'clock. (I've set the alarm clock.) We have to be at the airport for eight.

Answers:

Her brother (who arrived today) is coming tonight .

I like rock music (especially The Flying Saucers).

Hyphens

A hyphen is a short line used to link two or more words together to make one word or expression. You use a hyphen when you want to make sure the words are read as one:

A kind-hearted woman

Add hyphens to the following sentences to make them clearer.

She's good at do it yourself.

He received a long overdue award for his bravery.

It's only a short term arrangement.

She did mind boggling tricks.

Hyphens

Sometimes it's vital to use a hyphen because the meaning of a phrase changes without it:

Six-month-old boys
(boys who are six months old)

Six month-old boys
(six boys who are one month old)

Answers:

She's good at do-it-yourself.

He received a long-overdue award for his bravery.

It's only a short-term arrangement.

She did mind-boggling tricks.

3rd stop

Inverted commas

You use inverted commas to show the exact words someone has spoken. If the speech comes at the start of a sentence, it's followed by a comma, which goes inside the inverted commas:

"I always knew you were the murderer," said Inspector Green.

If the spoken words are at the end, put a comma before the speech begins:

Inspector Green said, "I always knew you were the murderer."

Add the commas and inverted commas to these sentences.

I'll see you tomorrow morning said Sam.

Kamani said I think I'll go to the beach today.

Inverted commas

If the spoken words are a question or an exclamation, you use a question mark or exclamation mark at the end of the speech, rather than a comma:

> **"How on earth did you catch the tiger?" asked Mrs Chan.**

> **"What a wonderful surprise!" said Adam.**

When you write the exact words someone has spoken, it's called "direct speech". See page 93 to find out about a different way to write speech.

Answers:

"I'll see you tomorrow morning," said Sam.

Kamani said, "I think I'll go to the beach today."

Reported speech

When you're writing what someone said, you can use reported speech rather than direct speech. (See page 91 for direct speech.) This means you just report what was said. So instead of this . . .

"I'm feeling ill," said Alicia to her sister.

. . . you would write this:

Alicia told her sister she was feeling ill.

Write these sentences in reported speech.

"I'm going to buy a new car," said Lily.

_____

_____

"Where are you going?" she asked him.

_____

_____

Reported speech

The tense of reported speech goes back one tense further than the tense of direct speech:

"I see it," he said.
becomes
He said that he saw it.

"I saw it," he said.
becomes
He said that he had seen it.

Answers:

"I'm going to buy a new car," said Lily.

Lily said she was going to buy a new car.

"Where are you going?" she asked him.

She asked him where he was going.

their/they're/there

It's very easy to get "their", "they're" and "there" mixed up, because they sound exactly the same.

"Their" means **"belonging to them"**.

"They're" is short for **"They are"**.

"There" describes where things are.

Choose the correct word to fill all the gaps.

I can see Mark and Lucie over

____.

with ____ dog, Archie.

____ are three girls in my class who are in a band. ____ always singing songs.

their / they're / there

"There" doesn't just mean "not here". It's also used with the verb "to be", in phrases like these:

There are bats in my attic.

There's a train in 20 minutes.

There are so many stars in the sky.

Answers:

I can see Mark and Lucie over _**there**_ . _**They're**_ with _**their**_ dog, Archie.

**There** are three girls in my class who are in a band. _**They're**_ always singing _**their**_ songs.

affect/effect

People often get "affect" and "effect" mixed up because they sound similar and mean similar things. But they're actually used in very different ways.

"Affect" is a verb:

The weather can affect the way you feel.

"Effect" is usually a noun:

The new medicine had a surprising effect.

Choose the correct word to fill all the gaps.

When I failed the exam, it _____ed my confidence.

What was the _____ of adding the blue powder?

affect/effect

Confusingly, "effect" is occasionally used as a verb rather than a noun. When used as a verb, it means "to bring about" or "to cause to happen":

The new coach effected a change in the team's results.

The magic spell effected a surprising transformation.

But remember, "affect" is always a verb, whereas "effect" is almost always used as a noun.

Answers:

When I failed the exam, it ___affect___ed my confidence.

What was the ___effect___ of adding the blue powder?

---

it's / its

People often confuse these two words, but they mean very different things.

it's

This is the shortened form of "it is".

its

This is a possessive adjective (see page 27) meaning "belonging to it":

the elephant wiggled its trunk.

Complete these sentences by adding the correct word in each space.

The rabbit ate _____ food.

_____ funny when a cat chases _____ tail.

I just saw the giant skyscraper and _____ amazing!

99

it's/its

"It's" can be short for "it has" as well as "it is":

It's nice that it's got warmer today.

Above, the first "it's" is short for "it is" and the second one is short for "it has". If you're not sure which word to use, try to say the sentence with "it is" or "it has". If it makes sense, you need an apostrophe.

Answers:

The rabbit ate ___its___ food.

___It's___ funny when a cat chases ___its___ tail.

I just saw the giant skyscraper and ___it's___ amazing!

who's / whose

It's very easy to get these two words mixed up because they sound the same.

who's

This is the shortened form of "who is" or "who has": the man who's staying with us.

whose

This is a relative pronoun which shows who something belongs to: the man whose house I'm staying at.

Fill the gaps with the correct word.

_____ **dog is this?**

Do you know _____

coming tonight?

Have you seen the man

_____ **hair is blue?**

who's/whose

When you're not sure which word to use, just say the sentence to yourself using either "who is" or "who has" – if the sentence still makes sense with one of those, then it's:

who's

But if the word shows who something belongs to, then it's:

whose

Answers:

Whose dog is this?

Do you know **who's** coming tonight?

Have you seen the man **whose** hair is blue?

you're/your

People often confuse these two words – they sound the same but mean totally different things.

you're
This is short for "you are".

your
This means "belonging to you".

Fill the blanks with the correct words.

_____ not going to spend

all _____ money, are you?

_____ a very good pianist.

I like _____ hair.

_____ my best friend.

you're/your

If you're not sure which word to use, just think about what you want to say. Try saying the sentence with "you are" – if it makes sense, then the word you need is:

you're

But if "you are" doesn't make sense, then the word you need means "belonging to you", so it's:

your

Answers:

__You're__ not going to spend all __your__ money, are you?

__You're__ a very good pianist.

I like __your__ hair.

__You're__ my best friend.

passed/past

People often confuse these two words, which sound the same.

passed

This word is only ever a verb: I have passed my exams.

past

This word can be used in lots of different ways (as a noun, adjective, preposition or adverb).

Add the correct word to each sentence.

She _____ me the parcel.

He cycled _____ the leader of the race.

As he _____ the stadium, he heard a huge cheer.

passed / past

With a sentence like this . . .

He cycled past the leader of the race.

. . . it's particularly easy to use "passed" by mistake. But remember: "passed" is only ever a verb. In the sentence above, "past" isn't a verb. If it were a verb, the sentence would read completely differently:

He passed the leader of the race on his bicycle.

Answers:

She __*passed*__ me the parcel.

He cycled __*past*__ the leader of the race.

As he __*passed*__ the stadium, he heard a huge cheer.

What you've learnt

On the next few pages you'll find a summary of all the grammar and punctuation rules in this book.

Types of words

Verbs (page 7) tell you what someone or something is doing.

Nouns (page 13) are name words. There are Common nouns (normal ones) and Proper nouns (page 15).

Adjectives (pages 23-25) tell you more about a noun. Possessive adjectives (page 27) show who something belongs to.

Adverbs (pages 29-31) tell you more about a verb or an adjective.

Pronouns (pages 17-21) are used instead of nouns to make a sentence less repetitive.

Prepositions (page 55) tell you how one thing relates to another.

Conjunctions (pages 67-68) link other words or groups of words together.

Verb tenses

To talk about the past, present, and future, we use different verb tenses. The most common tenses are the *present simple* (page 39), the *present continuous* (page 41), the *past simple* (page 43), and the *past continuous* (page 47). There are rules for using these tenses, but *irregular verbs* (page 45) don't follow the rules.

Sentences

Every sentence has a *subject* (page 9), a *verb* (page 7), and an *object* (page 11). Some sentences are broken up into sections called *clauses* (page 69). Some sentences use the *passive voice* (page 57).

Common mistakes

Here are some words that look or sound similar and can be confusing:

affect/effect (page 97)
it's/its (page 99)
passed/past (page 105)
their/they're/there (page 95)
who's/whose (page 101)
you're/your (page 103)

Punctuation marks

Punctuation marks are used to break up
your writing and make it easier to read.
Different punctuation marks have
different uses which help to make
your meaning clear.

These are the punctuation marks
that are covered in this book:

Index